Welcome to the ROYGBIV Pri...

ROYGBIV Print was created by parents, grandparents, uncles, aunts, god-parents, educators, and coaches. Our team believes in educating the future by helping our little ones develop motor skills and also help them explore their own creative potential. I

n addition, we believe in helping our kids learn and understand more about their own backgrounds, their friends' backgrounds, and the many other cultures that make up our great big world. ROYGBIV Print believes in adding more color to everyone's world, one page at a time!

We hope you can continue to support us and help us educate the world by leaving us a review on Amazon.com or sharing our work with your friends and family. If you're on Instagram, please follow us at @roygbivprint for updates on our future work! We love to hear comments and suggestions!

Thank you again!

-ROYGBIV Print

ROYGBIV
PRINT

Welcome to the ROYGBIV Print family!

ROYGBIV Print was created by parents, grandparents, uncles, aunts, god-parents, educators, and coaches like team others to educate the future by helping our little ones develop motor skills and also help them explore their own creative potential.

In addition, we believe in helping our kids learn and understand more about their own backgrounds, their friends' backgrounds, and the many other cultures that make up our great big world. ROYGBIV Print believes in adding more color to everyone's world, one page at a time!

We hope you can continue to support us and help us educate the world by leaving us a review on Amazon.com or sharing our work with your friends and family. If you're on Instagram, please follow us at @roygbivprint for updates on our future work! We love to hear comments and suggestions!

Thank you again!

-ROYGBIV Print

ROYGBIV

生肖
Shēngxiào
Zodiac

Shǔ
Rat

Niú

Ox

老虎

Lǎohǔ

Tiger

老虎

Lǎohǔ

Tiger

兔子

Tùzǐ

Rabbit

兔子

Tùzi

Rabbit

Lóng

Dragon

龍

Lóng

Dragon

Shé
Snake

蛇

Shé

Snake

馬

Mǎ

Horse

馬

Mǎ

Horse

Shānyáng
Goat

羊山

Shānyáng

Goat

Hóu

Monkey

Gǒu

Dog

ໝາ

Dog

公雞

Gōngjī

Rooster

gōngjī

Rooster

Zhū

Pig

Zhu

Pig

中國燈籠

Zhōngguó dēnglóng

Chinese Lantern

中国灯笼
Zhōngguó dēnglóng
Chinese Lantern

中國燈籠

Zhōngguó dēnglóng
Chinese Lantern

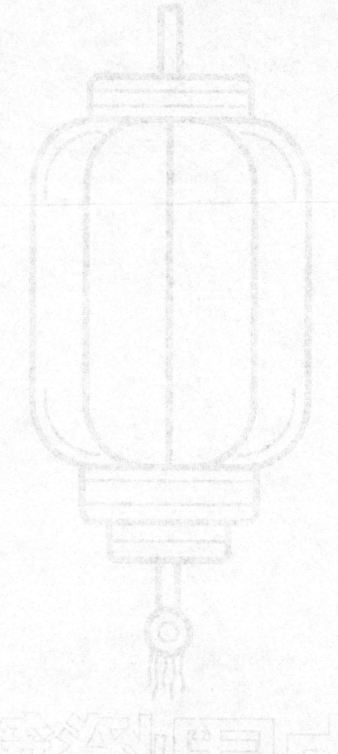

中国灯笼

Zhōngguó dēnglóng

Chinese Lantern

中國燈籠

Zhōngguó dēnglóng
Chinese Lantern

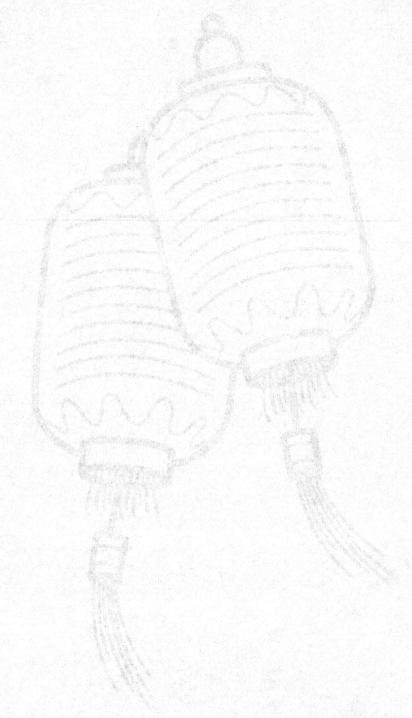

中国灯笼

Zhōngguó dēnglóng

Chinese Lantern

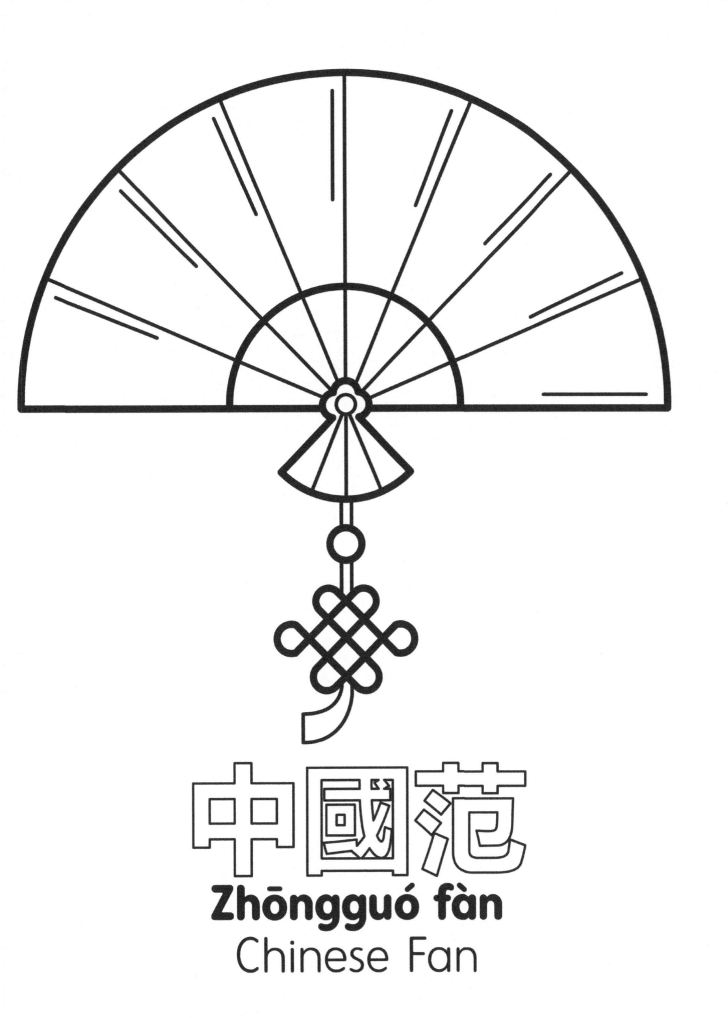

中國范

Zhōngguó fàn

Chinese Fan

中国扇

Zhōngguó fàn

Chinese fan

中國范

Zhōngguó fàn

Chinese Fan

中国扇

Zhōngguó fàn

Chinese fan

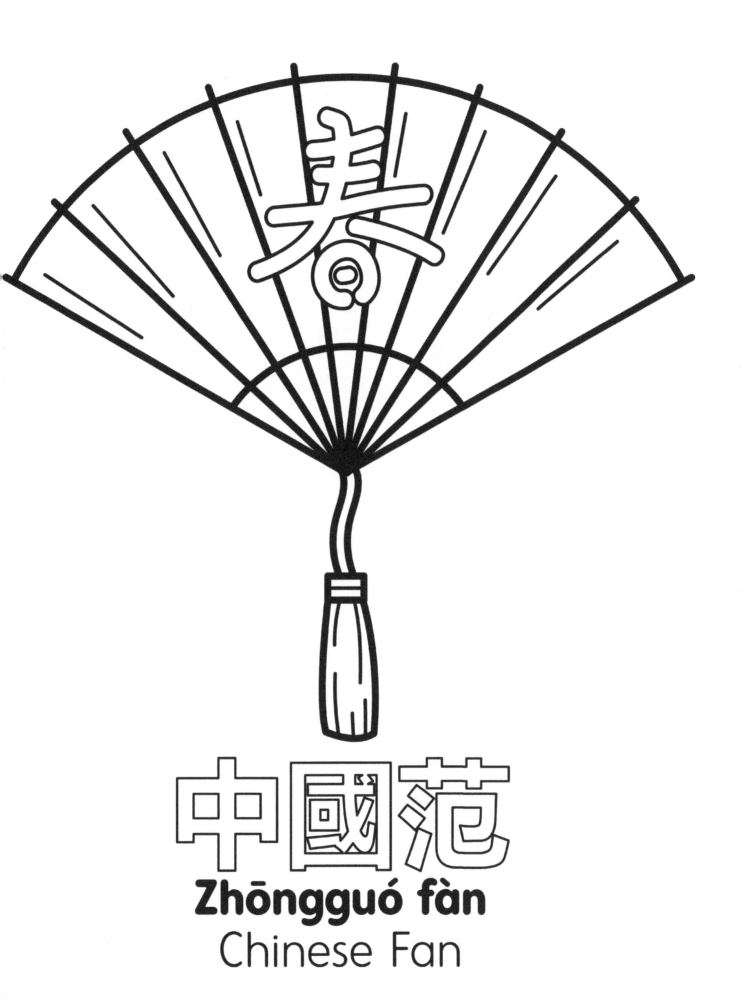

Zhōngguó fàn
Chinese Fan

中国扇
Zhōngguó fàn
Chinese fan

紅信封

Hóng xìnfēng

Red Envelope

红信封

Hóng xìnfēng

Red Envelope

紅信封

Hóng xìnfēng

Red Envelope

红信封
Hóng xìnfēng
Red Envelope

Xiāng

Chinese Incense

中國農曆新年

Zhōngguó nónglì xīnnián

Girl holding fireworks

中国融计新年

Zhōngguó róngjì xīnnián

girl holding fireworks

中國農曆新年
Zhōngguó nónglì xīnnián
Boy holding fireworks

中国农历新年

Zhōngguó nónglì xīnnián

Boy holding fireworks

舞狮师

Wǔ shī

Chinese Lion Dancer

Wǔ shī
Chinese Lion Dancer

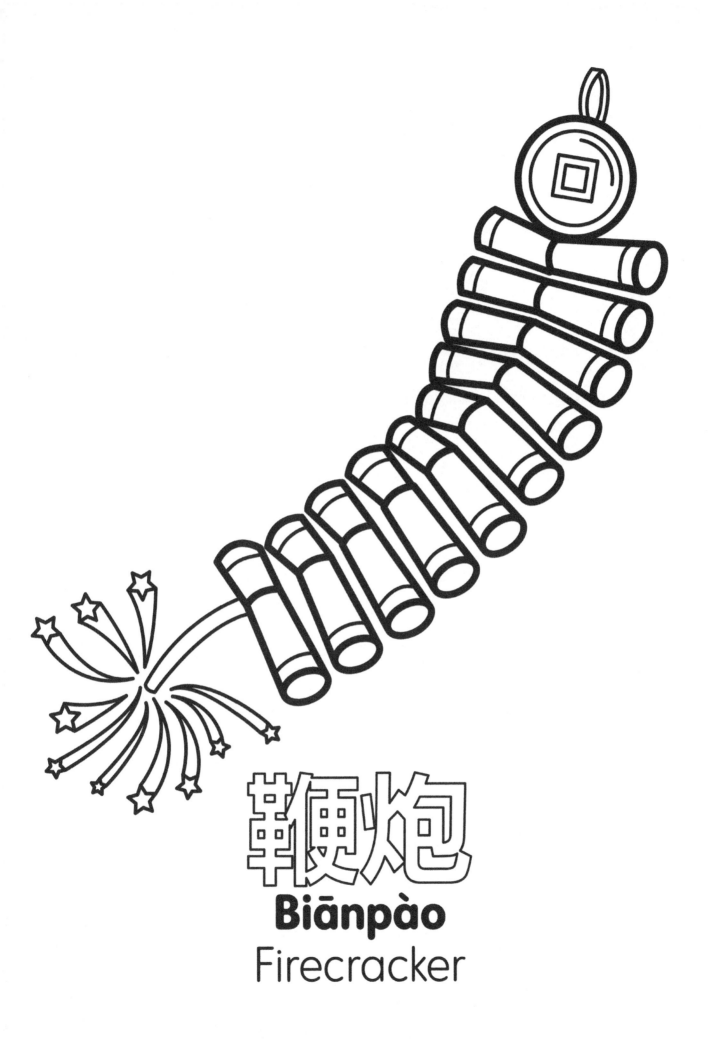

鞭炮

Biānpào

Firecracker

鞭炮

Bianpao

Firecracker

Wǔ shī

Chinese Lion

Wǔ shī

Chinese Lion

Wǔ shī

Chinese Lion

舞獅

Wǔ shī

Chinese lion

茶具

Chájù

Chinese tea set

茶具
Chájù
Chinese tea set

月餅

Yuèbǐng

Chinese Moon Cake

月餅
Yuèbǐng
Chinese Moon Cake

月餅

Yuèbǐng

Chinese Moon Cake

月饼
Yuèbǐng
Chinese Moon Cake

中秋節

Zhōngqiū jié

Mid-Autumn Festival

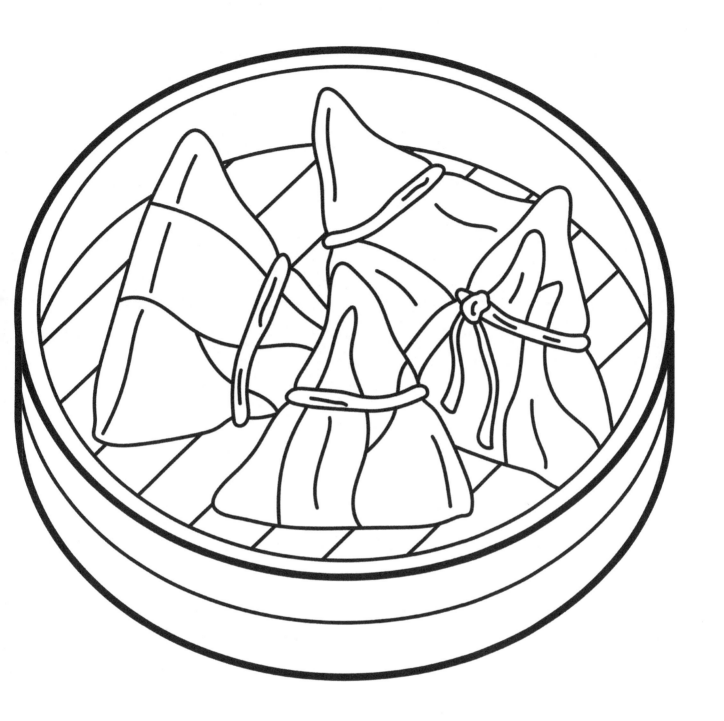

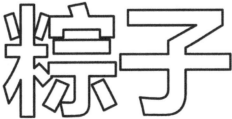

Zòngzi

Sticky Rice Dumplings

粽子

Zòngzi

Sticky Rice Dumplings

端午節
Duānwǔ jié
Chinese dragon boat

粽子

Zòngzi

Leaf Dumplings

粽子

Zòngzi

Leaf Dumplings

餃子

Jiǎozi

Dumplings

Jiǎozi
Dumplings

白菜

Báicài

Bok Choy

báicài

Bok Choy

蛋挞

Dàntà

Egg Tart

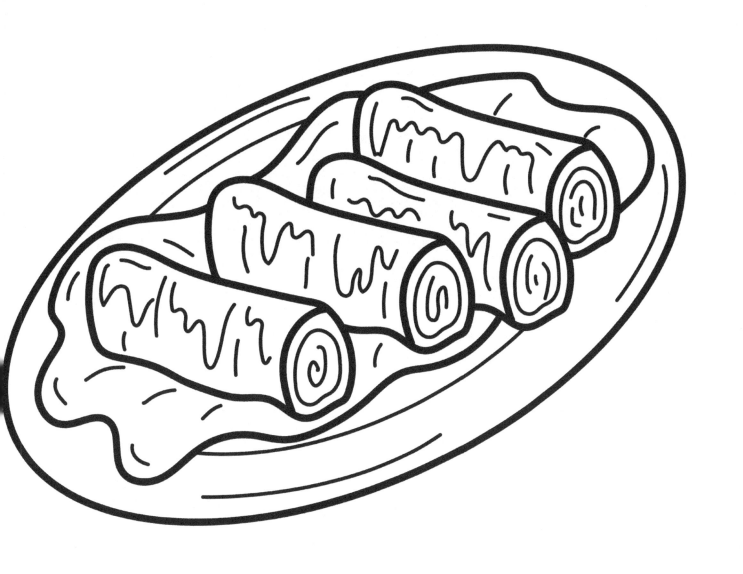

蛋捲
Dàn juǎn
Eggrolls

春卷

Dàn juǎn

Eggrolls

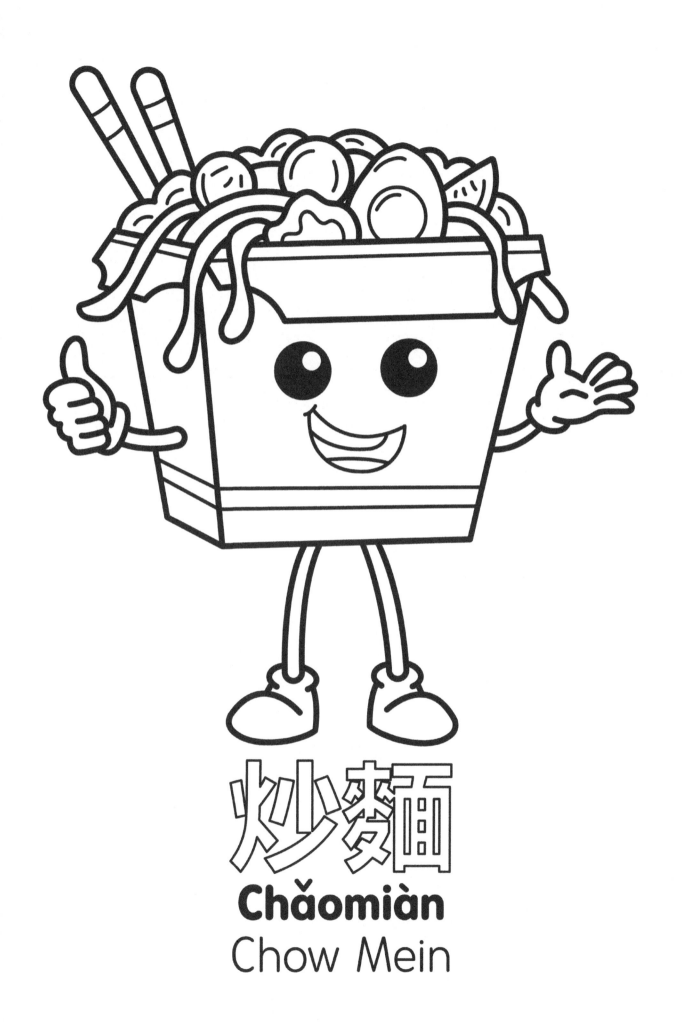

炒麵
Chǎomiàn
Chow Mein

Chǎomiàn
Chow Mein

麵湯
Miàntāng
Noodle Soup

煲仔飯

Bāo zǐ fàn

Claypot Rice

煲仔饭

Bāo zǐ fàn

Claypot Rice

筷子醬油

Kuài zǐ jiàngyóu

Chopstick and Soy Sauce

筷子醬油

Kuài zi jiàngyóu

Chopstick and Soy Sauce

家庭晚餐

Jiātíng wǎncān

Family Dinner

家庭晚餐

Jiātíng wǎncān

Family Dinner

Xióngmāo

Panda

Xiàngmāo
Panda

招財貓

Zhāocái māo

Lucky Cat

孫悟空/孙悟空

Sūnwùkōng
The Monkey King

孫悟空

Sunwukong

The Monkey King

Zhōngguó gōng

Chinese Palace

中国的长城
Zhōngguó de chángchéng
Great wall of China

中国的长城
Zhōngguó de chángchéng
Great wall of China

Yīnyáng

Yin and Yang

Yin and Yong

Made in the USA
Las Vegas, NV
07 February 2024

85418176R00057